LOOKING AT COUNTRIES

Looking at
NIGERIA

Jillian Powell

GARETH**STEVENS**
GS
PUBLISHING
A Member of the WRC Media Family of Companies

Please visit our web site at: www.garethstevens.com
For a free color catalog describing Gareth Stevens Publishing's list
of high-quality books and multimedia programs, call 1-800-542-2595 (USA)
or 1-800-387-3178 (Canada). Gareth Stevens Publishing's fax: (414) 332-3567.

Library of Congress Cataloging-in-Publication Data

Powell, Jillian.
   Looking at Nigeria / Jillian Powell.
      p. cm. — (Looking at countries)
   Includes index.
   ISBN-13: 978-0-8368-7671-0 (lib. bdg.)
   ISBN-13: 978-0-8368-7678-9 (softcover)
   1. Nigeria—Juvenile literature. I. Title.
   DT515.22.P69   2007
   966.9—dc22   2006035321

This North American edition first published in 2007 by
Gareth Stevens Publishing
A Member of the WRC Media Family of Companies
330 West Olive Street, Suite 100
Milwaukee, Wisconsin 53212 USA

This U.S. edition copyright © 2007 by Gareth Stevens, Inc.
Original edition copyright © 2006 by Franklin Watts.
First published in Great Britain in 2006 by Franklin Watts,
338 Euston Road, London NW1 3BH, United Kingdom.

Series editor: Sarah Peutrill
Art director: Jonathan Hair
Designer: Rita Storey
Picture research: Diana Morris

Gareth Stevens editor: Dorothy L. Gibbs
Gareth Stevens art direction: Tammy West
Gareth Stevens graphic designer: Charlie Dahl

Photo credits: (t=top, b=bottom, l=left, r=right, c=center)
Paul Almasy/Corbis: 22. Art Directors/TRIP: 4, 26tr. V. and M. Birley/Tropix: 16, 20t. Don Davis/Tropix: 7t, 27.
Eye Ubiquitous/Hutchison: 8, 10, 14. Werner Forman/Corbis: 18bl. Kerstin Geier/Gallo Images/Corbis: 19. Liz Gilbert/
Sygma/Corbis: 18tr. Martin Harvey/Still Pictures: 6. Ed Kashi/Corbis: 24. M. MacDonald/Tropix: 7b. James Marshall/
Corbis: 23b. Marcel Mettelsiefen/epa/Corbis: 9, 15. Giacomo Pirozzi/Panos: 12. Betty Press/Panos: 17, 20b. Jacob
Silberberg/Panos: 1, 11b, 23t. Superbild/A1 Pix: front cover, 11t, 25, 26bl. Liba Taylor/Corbis: 13, 21.

Printed in Canada

1 2 3 4 5 6 7 8 9 10 10 09 08 07 06

Contents

Words that appear in the glossary are printed in **boldface** type the first time they occur in the text.

Where is Nigeria?

Nigeria is in western Africa. It shares borders with four other African countries and has a coastline on the Gulf of Guinea, in the Atlantic Ocean.

The capital city of Nigeria is Abuja. It is right in the middle of the country. Abuja became Nigeria's capital in 1991, when government offices moved there from Lagos. It is the fastest-growing city in Africa.

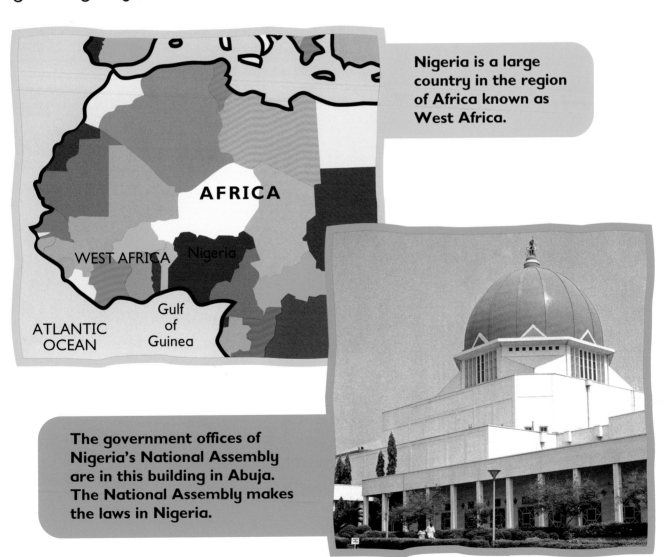

AFRICA

WEST AFRICA

Nigeria

Gulf of Guinea

ATLANTIC OCEAN

Nigeria is a large country in the region of Africa known as West Africa.

The government offices of Nigeria's National Assembly are in this building in Abuja. The National Assembly makes the laws in Nigeria.

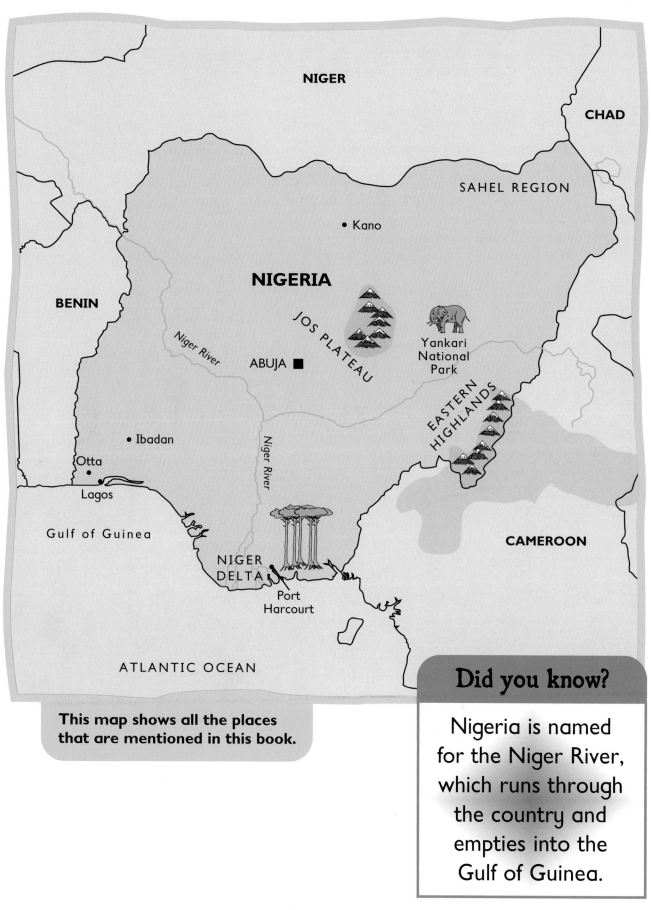

NIGER

CHAD

SAHEL REGION

• Kano

NIGERIA

BENIN

Niger River

JOS PLATEAU

ABUJA ■

Yankari
National
Park

EASTERN
HIGHLANDS

Niger River

• Ibadan

Otta
•

Lagos

Gulf of Guinea

CAMEROON

NIGER
DELTA

Port
Harcourt

ATLANTIC OCEAN

**This map shows all the places
that are mentioned in this book.**

Did you know?

Nigeria is named
for the Niger River,
which runs through
the country and
empties into the
Gulf of Guinea.

The Landscape

Nigeria's variety of landscapes include the flat, grassy plains of the **savanna**, thick **tropical** rain forests, and saltwater swamps. The country also has some mountains, on the Jos **Plateau**, in central Nigeria, and in the eastern highlands, on the border with Cameroon.

The landscape over much of Nigeria is savanna grasslands.

Dust storms are common in the dry, northeastern Sahel region.

Mangroves grow well in the delta region on the southern coast of Nigeria.

In the far northeast, called the Sahel region, the land is dry and dusty. This region is at the edge of the Sahara Desert.

Swampy **mangrove** forests grow along the south coast of Nigeria, near the Niger **delta**.

Did you know?

Sahel is an Arabic word that means "border."

Weather and Seasons

Nigeria has only two seasons. The rainy season lasts from April to October. The rest of the year is the dry season. In the south, Nigeria's weather is tropical, and temperatures are hot all year.

In central Nigeria, the weather is hot and humid during the rainy season but cooler and drier during the dry season.

The hilly landscape and high **altitude** of the countryside around Zuma Rock, in Abuja, help keep temperatures **moderate** during the dry season.

To the people of Nigeria, a drought means not having enough food and water. Charities often set up special places where people can get safe water to drink.

The driest weather is in the north, where days are hot and nights are cool. Here, the rainy season lasts from April to September. When the rains come late, there can be **droughts**. During the dry season, between December and March, a strong wind called the harmattan blows in from the Sahara Desert.

Did you know?

About half the people in Nigeria have a difficult time getting safe drinking water.

9

Nigerian People

Nigeria is known as "the giant of Africa" because it has more than 150 million people. Nigeria has the largest **population** of any African country.

Nigeria's population includes more than 250 different groups of peoples. Each group has its own **traditions**, language, and religion. The main groups are the Hausa and the Fulani in the north, the Yoruba in the southwest, and the Igbo in the southeast.

The Fulani people herd cows. The animals provide the Fulani with meat and milk.

Religion is an important part of life in Nigeria. Most Nigerians are Muslims or Christians, but some follow native African religions. In these religions, people worship the spirits of **ancestors** or a variety of gods and goddesses.

This man is decorating a white horse for a special Muslim festival.

Singing is part of this Christmas Day service at a Christian church in Otta.

School and Family

Children in Nigeria spend twelve years in school. Then, some of them go on to colleges, universities, or trade schools. Many Nigerian schools and colleges now have computers so their students can learn the skills they need to find good jobs.

Most Nigerian children go to school, but there are still about 12 million of them who do not go to school. They have to work to help bring in money for their families. Some of them get money by selling water or snack foods on the streets.

Many primary schoolchildren in Nigeria gather together each morning to sing.

These Nigerian college students are learning computer skills.

Many families in Nigeria are large. Parents often have six or seven children. Children are important in family life. For some Nigerian families, having many children means more help in the fields. Even children who go to school, help out at home or in the fields after school and on holidays.

Did you know?

In Nigeria, children are not usually given a name until the eighth day after they are born.

Country Life

Most people in Nigeria live in the countryside. Often, all the relatives in a family live close together in the same village. Related families live in groups of houses called **compounds**. From parents and grandparents to uncles, aunts, and children, everyone plays a part in family life.

Did you know?

Bicycles are used as taxis in countryside areas of Nigeria. One bicycle can carry up to four people.

These people are all relatives from one big family, and they all live together in the same village.

In a countryside village in Nigeria, cooking often starts with pounding cassava to make a type of flour. Cassava is a starchy root vegetable that grows undergraund, like a potato.

Most of the men who live in countryside villages work in the fields around the village. The women take care of vegetable gardens and animals such as goats, chickens, and pigs. Village women also do all the cooking.

Sometimes, especially in the south, village women earn money by selling vegetables or cloth at markets. Some Yoruba people and Igbo people also make pottery, masks, and bead- or metalwork to sell to tourists at the markets.

15

City Life

The cities in Nigeria are growing quickly because many people have been moving away from the countryside to work in the cities. The largest Nigerian cities are Lagos, Kano, and Ibadan. The capital city, Abuja, is much smaller than other Nigerian cities, but it still has many industries, shops, and hotels, as well as an international airport.

Richer people in Nigerian cities live in houses behind walls and gates. These houses are in Port Harcourt.

Lagos, which was the capital of Nigeria before Abuja, has a population of more than 12 million people. Although Abuja is now the capital, Lagos is still an important business center.

This street in Lagos is crowded with people, buses, and taxis.

Like many big cities, Lagos has to deal with problems such as traffic, overcrowding, and pollution. Lagos has other problems, too. During the rainy season, the streets are often flooded, and during the dry season, the city often does not have enough water. During the dry season, many people in Lagos have to buy water.

Did you know?

Nigerian cities are some of the fastest-growing cities in Africa.

Nigerian Houses

In Nigeria's cities, many people live in large apartment buildings. Only the richest people have modern houses. The poorest people live in **shantytowns** called popular settlements. Their poorly built houses are made from scraps of tin and wood.

These modern apartment buildings are in Lagos.

This mud house in Kano is decorated with a carving.

In the old city of Kano, in northern Nigeria, houses are built out of mud bricks and are decorated with pictures. New houses are sometimes built in the old style, but they are made of concrete instead of mud.

This Nigerian boy is standing in front of a building that stores grain. In a countryside village, groups of houses share a grain store and a toilet.

Many of the houses in countryside villages are built using mud bricks, clay, or wood and have roofs made of palm or reed **thatch**. In the swampy delta region, houses are built high on stilts to keep them from being flooded. Village houses have no electricity, and water has to be **fetched** from a well.

Did you know?

Mud bricks keep houses cool during the day and warm at night.

Nigerian Food

Food is a central part of family life in Nigeria. Although fast foods are becoming popular, many Nigerians still cook at home for their families and friends and buy foods such as rice, cereals, and spices at local markets.

Many people in Nigerian cities and towns shop at discount, or low-price, food stores.

Women and children from countryside villages sell vegetables at city markets.

Rice, corn, and many other grains are sold by weight at Nigerian markets.

Did you know?

Cassava and yams, or sweet potatoes, are high in vitamin C, which helps fight germs and prevent illnesses.

Cassava and yams are important foods in Nigerian cooking. They are made into flour that is used to thicken soups and stews. These dishes often contain fish, or meat such as chicken, beef, or goat. Nigerians also eat a lot of vegetables, especially tomatoes, onions, and peppers, and many kinds of tropical fruits.

At Work

Most people in the countryside work in farming or fishing. Farmers have small plots of land where they grow enough for their families to eat and, sometimes, a little extra to sell. In the south, many farm workers have jobs on big plantations that grow cocoa or nuts to sell to other countries.

In cities, many people work in factories or offices or sell goods at markets or from street stalls. During traffic jams, some people go right into the streets trying to sell goods such as videos and televisions to people in their cars.

This man works at a market in Kano. He is selling cloth made from Nigerian cotton.

Oil and natural gas are two of Nigeria's most important industries. Other industries include processing foods and **manufacturing** cement, plastics, paper, **textiles**, car parts, and medicines.

The people at this busy office in Lagos are working for a daily newspaper.

This worker is checking **equipment** at a natural gas plant in southern Nigeria.

Did you know?

Nigeria is the largest oil producer in Africa and the eighth largest in the world.

Having Fun

Nigerians, young and old, enjoy watching and playing sports and games. Soccer, volleyball, wrestling, and boxing are all popular sports in Nigeria. *Ayo* is a favorite traditional game that can be played with objects as simple as seeds and cups. The children in Nigeria like to play hand-clapping games.

Almost every town and village in Nigeria has a place to play soccer. These boys are playing a game of soccer next to an oil refinery.

This **masquerade** dancer is part of the celebration at a Yoruba festival.

Thoughout the year, Nigeria has many colorful festivals. Some are Muslim or Christian religious celebrations. Others honor African gods or ancestors or the harvests of crops or fish.

Feasting, drumming, and dancing are part of festival celebrations in Nigeria. Some festival dancers dress in special costumes and masks. Nigerian festivals often have wrestling matches or boat races to watch, too.

Did you know?

The pop music of West Africa is called highlife music. It is **jazzy** music, played mainly on horns and guitars.

25

Nigeria: The Facts

- Nigeria is a **federal republic**. It is also a member of the **Commonwealth of Nations**.

- The president is the head of the government.

- The country is divided into thirty-six states, plus the area of the capital city, Abuja, which is called the Federal Capital Territory.

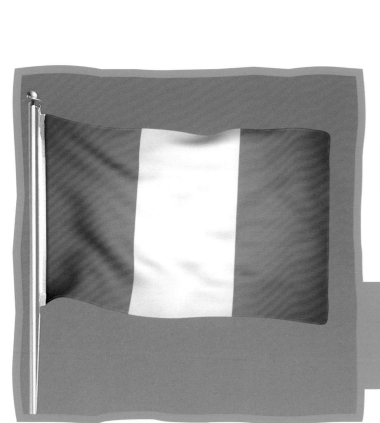

Nigerian currency is called naira. The currency above shows 5, 10, and 50 naira notes.

The Nigerian flag has bands of green, for its rich land, on each side of a white band, which stands for peace.

An African elephant is one of many wild animals to be seen in the Yankari National Park in eastern Nigeria.

- Nigeria has eight national parks. These parks help protect the country's land and animals. The parks also attract tourists.

- Each year, on October 1, Nigerians remember the day their country gained independence from Britain, in 1960. On this day, the president makes a speech, and people all over Nigeria join in parades and celebrations to honor this event.

Did you know?

Each of Nigeria's thirty-six states has its own radio station.

27

Glossary

altitude – the distance or height above sea level

ancestors – family members who lived in the past

Commonwealth of Nations – a group of independent countries that were once ruled by Great Britain

compounds – groups of houses, often built close together in a fenced-in area, that share many facilities and resources

delta – a triangular area of land formed by a river as it spreads out and flows into a sea or an ocean

droughts – long periods of time without rain that are harmful to plants and animals in the area

equipment – the machines and other tools needed to do a job or to make something work

federal republic – a kind of government in which decisions are made by the people of the country's states and regions and the people they vote to represent them

fetched – found somewhere else and brought back

jazzy – having jazz-style rhythms

mangrove – a tropical tree that grows in saltwater along seacoasts and has stiltlike roots growing out of its branches

manufacturing – making something in a factory

masquerade – wearing a costume or a mask to appear to be someone or something else

moderate – not too hot or not too cold

plateau – a large area of high, flat ground

population – the official count of the number of people in an area

savanna – a large area of treeless grassland in a tropical region

shantytowns – crowded, dirty places where poor people live in run-down houses

textiles – threads, yarns, woven materials and cloths, or fabrics

thatch – plant material, such as grass, straw, or branches, used as a protective covering

traditions – the ways of living and beliefs of certain people that have been passed down through generations

tropical – describing the warm, wet regions of Earth that are close to the equator

Find Out More

Kids Zone: Nigeria
www.afro.com/children/discover/nigeria/nigeria.html

Time for Kids: Nigeria
www.timeforkids.com/TFK/hh/goplaces/main/
   0,20344,1044380,00.html

ZoomSchool Africa: Africa's Geography
www.EnchantedLearning.com/school/Africa/Africamap.shtml

Publisher's note to educators and parents: Our editors have carefully reviewed these Web sites to ensure that they are suitable for children. Many Web sites change frequently, however, and we cannot guarantee that a site's future contents will continue to meet our high standards of quality and educational value. Be advised that children should be closely supervised whenever they access the Internet.

My Map of Nigeria

Photocopy or trace the map on page 31. Then write in the names of the countries, cities, bodies of water, and land areas and parks listed below. (Look at the map on page 5 if you need help.)

After you have written in the names of all the places, find some crayons and color the map!

Countries
Benin
Cameroon
Chad
Niger
Nigeria

Cities
Abuja
Ibadan
Kano
Lagos
Otta
Port Harcourt

Bodies of Water
Atlantic Ocean
Gulf of Guinea
Niger River

Land Areas and Parks
Eastern Highlands
Jos Plateau
Niger Delta
Sahel Region
Yankari National Park

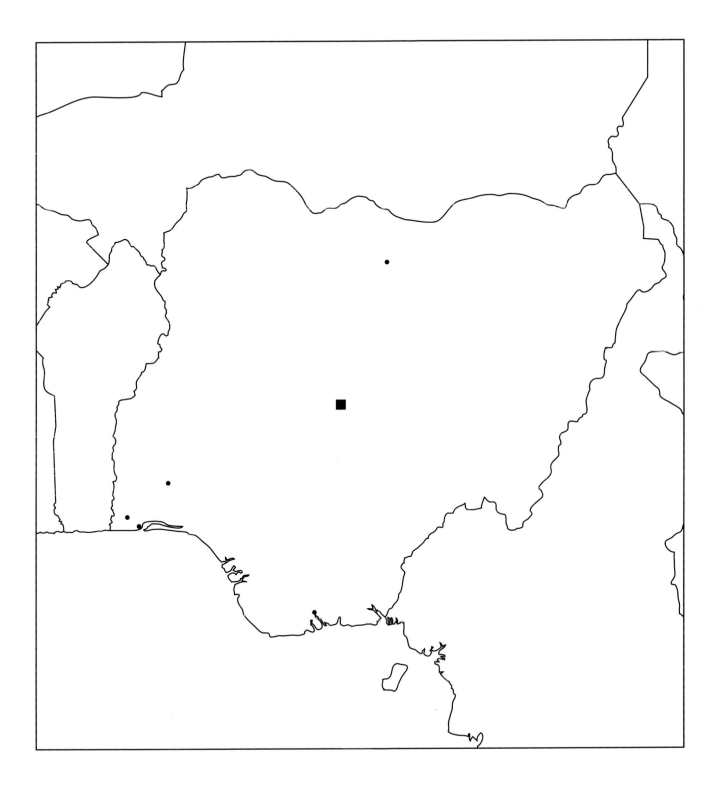

Index